M000305612

The

Sound of Silence

May Reign

First published by Marianne Ritchey (May Reign)

Front cover photo by A Freeman Photography

Back cover photo by Marianne Ritchey

Printed in the United States of America

Cover and interior design: Raven Tree Design

This book is dedicated to my mother, Ozzie Mae Ritchey
because she taught me that a woman can be feminine,
powerful and equal. She is a feminist by design.
Everything I know about authority, love, faith, and survival,
I learned from her...I have her hands.

Contents

Foreword

Dr. Maya Angelou's poignant quote "I've learned that people will forget what you said, people will forget what you did, but people will never forget how you made them feel" had never been driven home for me more clearly than when May Reign honored me by asking if I would write the Foreword for "The Sound of Silence". I cannot tell you when I met May Reign or even the circumstances that allowed us to make each other's acquaintance, but I remember how she made me feel so many things; anxious, uncomfortable and intrigued. It was very apparent to me that she was determined to live out loud, quietly. It seemed that her presence and actions were considerably stronger than her actual voice, so I was never able to anticipate what was coming next with her. She gave no warnings. My anxiety was the perfect fuel for her sense of humor and she delighted in seeing me squirm whenever she would say the unexpected.

Nothing was more unexpected than the first time I heard her recite. Her poem was titled Sally Hemmings. There stood the surreptitiously bold chick who could fly under the radar with her wit and observations (if you were dumb enough to not pay attention) astounding me with her solid stage presence and charged lyricism. I wasn't ready, I was never ready for May Reign. That was also the first time I heard her sing. I remember thinking "She don' messed up, because she is going to have to sing that for me on command every time I demand it." I figured it would be a fair exchange for her relentless teasing. I can hear her singing as I type this – clear and assured, "You live and you die…spend the years in between asking the question why…you've been through what you've been…"

For me, it felt like the earth stopped spinning on its axis. I suppose it was then that I knew that this is what she would always do – just show up and show out. That's exactly what she's been doing. Leave the pomp and circumstance to those who require validation to plan their next move. May Reign will let you know about it when it's time for YOU to be about it. I didn't know this book was being written until I was asked to fit in this final piece of the puzzle.

In another poem of hers, the verse is – "I just want him to know, that emotions planted so deep can only grow. I just want him to know, that I ain't scared no mo', and I'm ready, for love." Five words within that verse grabbed me "I ain't scared no mo". Again, that quiet confidence. Not loudly proclaimed, or unnecessarily emphasized, no. It was a confident confirmation, for herself and for anyone wondering, I ain't scared no mo. I remember being acutely aware of her lightly pronounced exhalation, a sigh of satisfaction if you will as she spoke those particular words. It made me want to be unafraid, too.

So yeah, I had to write May Reign to confirm her poetry lyrics, to make sure I had the song lyrics right in order to complete this.

I feel like I shouldn't have had to ask her anything, because - how does one allow themselves to forget a single detail of a friendship that has been as solid as her poetry? I managed to forget too many of those details. I may not be able to tell you the first words spoken between us, but I can promise you that I will never forget how she made me feel. May this book be exactly that, for you.

Terri A. Meredith
ILLESTrator/Retired Spoken Word Artist

Scarred (Haiku)

Born adventurous,

Used to skate with no kneepads-

But scars, change people.

Roses

Agonizing loneliness but,
single ladies appear luxurious
In the distance
I forget-
Not to take love for granted.
Enchanted,
I forget to remember
feeling dismembered
Disconnected
From love
I forgot who I was.
As cold as ice or isolation,
I vent for ventilation
I begged not to be loved

Insanity became my normalcy

The responsibility too much for me,

to read between the lines

to read into the minds of lovers.

I despised the perplexities of whether to share or listen

Trying to create closeness in the distance

Trying to find the rhythm

In their mathematical theorems

The moments of silence

As heavy as violence

Screams going unheard

Speaking, with the absence of words

Person without personality

I blamed love for what hatred did to me

I am a woman scorned

Burned with love learned and unlearned.

Though I appear strong,

My history is long

And deep be the scars

Of this broken heart

These are the cries of my soul

Are you listening?

My independence

is a mechanism of defense

I straddle thee fence

Some days wanting closeness,

Some days aloof.

Some days, speaking truth

Some days, under false pretense

I wake up needing rest

I fall asleep in the darkness

Masturbating with loneliness,

the only intimacy I have known

wondering how is it that I give all of me

and in return they leave me torn.

It seems that everyone wants my roses,

But they cannot embrace my thorns.

It seems that everyone wants my roses but they cannot-

Hunger Pains

In the morning-

I can still TASTE your glaze on my lips.

Nothing satisfies me like this.

I hide my insecurities in our intimacy.

Your SWEETNESS is surely my weakness.

You take precedence over everything good for me

because you are good to me.

And yes this is dysfunctional

But I am human

and EMOTIONAL.

I INDULGE, to diverge a deeper HUNGER.

Your presence,

quenches my loneliness.

So I assume that I can CONSUME you

til I am FULL;

or too disillusioned to acknowledge my emptiness.

Beneath my dress,

I camouflage my imperfections.

I hide from my reflection.

But you,

you love my nakedness,

Love to see me SPREADING,

regretting, dreading this ADDICTION

that hides my affliction.

I turn,

and see the broken WRAPPER,

the evidence of your DECADENCE.

I lay in reverence.

As you are the only certainty I know.

But truth is,

you do not love me.

You are a temporary fix to my brokenness.

You FEED me lies

With no NUTRITIONAL value,

And your presence

has become necessary

because nothing fills emptiness like GLUTTONY.

But this RELATIONSHIP

is not HEALTHY.

And these momentary burst of

satisfaction cannot ever truly make me happy.

So I am done,

done with cupcakes, candy, and yes honey buns!

Done with the misconception to which you allude.

The way you control my cycle;

the way you influence my mood,

this false sense of security that I create with FOOD.

Sometimes in the turbulence

I await loss.

Causing me to struggle with weight loss.

And yes sometimes it's easier to DIGEST a treat,

than to digress and accept defeat.

So I EAT.

Not realizing that COMFORT FOOD has been mechanically
     tweaked.

Scientist adding ingredients

To keep me obedient and subservient-

With diabetes on the rise,

they invent new pies

with new lies

and bright packages

to appear more attractive,

senses stimulated and reactive

but the fact is,

you are, what you consume.

From the kitchen to the bedroom.

This love affair that I've had with FOOD is over.

It's not you, it's me.

Sincerely,

The emotional eater

Woman (6 word story)

She will

Die trying

To live

When the Bird Breaks Free
(Thinking of Maya)

And talk about caged birds singing

Or rather church bells ringing

Or moments in your upbringing

that somehow last a life time.

Leave you reaching for a life line,

Until the right rhyme

Separates the thin line

Between living

And surviving

Breathing and learning to exhale

Growing strong in moments that left you frail

and fragile

Like a small child

That ran and hid beneath their eyelids

Cause I did,

Get lost in my adolescence.

Stripped of my innocence

Viewing the world

from different sides and three eyes

And nine lives

And real lies and realized

That still I rise

Like sun rises

Whether you love me or not.

Never mind your preference

Truth be my only source of reference

And self love is my defense mechanism

So I fight for my writes

Like my life depends on pens.

On pins and needles,

I teach my daughter bout the-

birds and beetles

What honey?

We are not B's

We are Queens.

That Quest Love

like Roots

That seeks light

like fruit

We are growing like flowers

Our hearts are gardens

Extreme drought

Makes us hardened

And thirsting

Libation

I been the Mrs. and the mistress

The Good morning and the Goodnight kisses

The fix

And the fixture

The prescription and the ailment

The rider

And the derailment

These ain't poems

These are memoirs

And these are war scars,

stretch marks

This is writing to the moonlight

Cause the lights off

Not cause it's romantic

This is my low points

But you've never seen me frantic

If you can't see where I been

Then you can't see where I'm destined

If you can't see this struggle

Then you'll never understand my blessins

And my questions

have been the only answers I know.

When the roots choked me lifeless

I still found a way to grow.

I be the fruit of my mother's truth

And my father's harsh delivery.

I be deep as ancestry.

Authentic by bloodline.

Prolific by design.

They invite me to keep silent.

Humbly I declined.

Most don't get my meaning.

See, I cannot be defined.

Phenomenal be this woman

My evolution on incline

Gone be the days of acrobatics

I was not made to bend

Self expression be my birthright

I was not created to blend

I stand out, just by standing.

I don't know how to fit in.

I too, was once a caged bird,

I found that freedom is

achieved once received from within.

Justice for Our Sons

Y'all don't wanna hold picket signs cause we got gel nails to think
    about.

Y'all ain't tryin' to march cause y'all shoe game so vicious.

And if you turn a blind eye and don't look,

then you don't look suspicious.

Turn down for what!

We taking Tequila shots to the head

and they taking fatal shots to their heads.

It's like the news is on repeat, another black boy dead.

While our fight stays confined to our Facebook post

They're building prisons and boats

Cause this must be how the slave trade took place.

Killin' our babies in our face

And daring us to react.

Matter of fact, you niggas stand back

Cause we blastin' anything that's black.

Using our sons as target practice.

Eye witnesses

but they still manage to distort what the facts is.

And we pay their salary with our taxes.

After Trayvon, I told my son he can't wear his hoodie no more.

And now I'll just tell him not to walk, run or breathe.

Cause anybody wit' a badge on his chest

got tricks up his sleeve.

Being a black boy is like suicide in our society.

The KKK ain't always in white sheets.

Now they're in uniforms patrolling our streets.

Rosa didn't get out of her seat-

Cause she knew this day was coming.

A black man ran for President but they still got my people running.

Our babies are becoming-endangered species.

Treated like feces.

Cause the police be

trigger happy,

and hypersensitive.

Ready to erase the bright future of a black kid.

Don't matter if he's unarmed.

They don't walk away unharmed.

We are tired and broken hearted.

Unheard and disregarded.

We cannot raise strong black men

If they must walk subservient.

We cannot expect them to be good citizens

if they fear lights and sirens.

Oppression will only ignite their aggression.

Our people cannot digest digression.

We've come too far-

from walking barefoot in the dark,

 guided only by the stars.

But we must remember who we are.

Remember the hurt,

run our fingers across these historical scars.

I don't wanna sing no more negro spirituals.

I don't wanna attend no more vigils for innocent individuals.

We see your aim, and if our children are your target,

Let us re-emerge the Black Panther Party.

Feels like they are waging war.

So I'm feeling like Assata Shakur.

Cause I gotta young black boy that I'm willing to die for.

I'm tired

And when my son is the prey,

Then I ain't prayin' no more.

-For Michael Brown, for Trayvon Martin,

for Eric Garner, and for all the young black males

who died at the hand of racism, inequality, and injustice.

Purpose (Haiku)

You should never live

Above your means, but rather-

A life with meaning

Day One (Haiku)

You are not one I-
Fully know right now, but hey
I'm still learning me.

While You Were Out

One day I noticed a pretty face

when you needed space

And I couldn't take

the emptiness no more.

Though nothing physical about our ritual,

she sees this open door.

We certainly exchange intimacies,

And I have the tendency

To miss her like this short time

is forever,

Or at least I want it to be.

We share stories

Of frustration

And thirst and lonely days,

Like where has she been all of my Sundays

When I wanted to love easily

Sleep in late

After date night

Cause sometimes I hate nights

I hate fights

That end up with ended calls

And me staring at white walls

When darkness falls

Because the distance

Is further than we'd like to admit

And now this.

I-

Notice I don't fuss about missed calls anymore

In fact tonight it's what I hoped for

Because somewhere in this distance

I'm feeling closer to a stranger

Because the heart is a karma-chameleon

Evolving with experience and regimen

In the midst of your absence

she has my attention

And that...scares me.

My heart dares me to walk away,

Not to be with her

But just to be- with her

Freeing myself from such uncertainty

As what could it hurt to see

If her courtesy or just holding me is

anywhere in my destiny

Today she is just a face to replace a space that is empty.

Yet we exchange energy and spiritual chemistry-

And I'm intrigued to say the least.

While you were out,

She said she's really IN to me.

Intimacy (Haiku)

When you allow me

To take in your energy

Then we have made love.

Skin Deep (Haiku)

To breathe in, your air

To hear your thoughts with my heart

Is deeper than touch

Love Language

Love,

A continual thing,

embraced by both of us.

Squeezing, only as tightly as you want to be held.

Giving what you prayed for.

No keeping score,

Not blindly

But with insight

And intensity

With volume and density-

With freedom and sincerity.

Balancing and grasping.

Breathing and not simply because there are lungs.

But breathing the same air

Simultaneously

Now that's life support.

Not by default

Rather like vaults

Hiding our faults

Both sacred

Not jaded,

or weighted.

Rather like you waited for this.

Like I be the only cure

for your loneliness.

Protecting each other.

Because we are more

than lovers.

We blend like friends

Oh baby I like it raw.

I mean fresh fruit

I need my lovin' organic

With urgency

As if losing me

Could cause panic

Like losing your keys

When you got somewhere to be

I want you to remember how long you searched for me.

I want you to move Heaven and Earth for me

Cause you be God-like

I wanna feel like God's wife.

Like you would give your life-

to preserve my innocence.

I wanna hear angels cry

when we're intimate.

Like this be infinite

I wanna get into it

like intuition.

Hide me in your heart.

It is the safest place I have known.

I had grown

too comfortable in empty spaces.

And desolate places become decorative.

I shared my deepest secrets with the darkness.

I screamed loudest in my silence.

Loneliness is the worst kind of domestic violence.

So I wanna feel safe with you.

Simply put, I wanna feel great with you.

I wanna know that you get me.

I wanna know that you got me.

When the weight is heavy on my shoulders

I wanna know that you'll spot me.

We may not always speak the same love language,

but I need to know that before you leave me alone,

you'll buy the whole audio collection of Rosetta Stone.

At least trying,

At least.

Treats (Haiku)

They say men are dogs

So then I bought me a dog

Wasn't hard to train

Love Poem

I feel like writing a love poem, about how I hate love

So I guess it's a hate poem

I guess its back to porn

Like fuck love I'm scorned

Like this is THAT poem.

This is so redundant

I want my time refunded

I want back my kiss,

my lovemaking and sexual gifts

My Saturday afternoons

The smell of my perfume.

I want you to send back my sweetness,

that you mistake for weakness

I want my weekends,

mailed back to me,

before the week

ends.

I'm tired of giving, so I give in.

You think that because your baggage is name brand,

I should gladly carry it.

I guess I should stop hoping

for horses and chariots.

There is no matrimony in masquerades.

And I can see your charades.

I recognize your false pretense

Asking for closeness while creating distance

I can see clearly,

in retrospect,

I still prayed for a Revolution

Now you truly be my Malcolm, ex.

I loved you by any means necessary.

You give me mediocrity

While promising extraordinary

I'm tired of the lies

I'm tired of your X,

I'm tired of the whys.

I fell in love with your disguise.

I can hear the answers in my questions.

I can feel the accuracy in your regression.

So I, had a heart to heart with me

Realized that the definition of this insanity,

Is ignoring red flags

And expecting no penalties

All is fair in love and war

But if winning you, means losing me

Then who is really keeping score?

I look in your eyes,

Wondering how many empty promises you got left.

I walk away, tired of holding my breath

Reminded that what I ask of you,

I had never given myself.

I promised that last time

was gonna be the LAST time

I'd fall in love with my own expectations.

I promised I'd slow down to venture past representation,

I promised I'd allow reputation to be built by repetition

But my need to be needed, superseded

Aborted my mission

And I found myself dancing to this rendition

Of a love song,

even after the melody was gone.

Today I questioned my choice to walk away.

But then again, this is running, from what's coming.

I can smell the rain.

I can feel the pain.

I'd be foolish to await the incision,

while soothing your apprehensions.

These illusions you paint are blurred and faint

Nothing clear, nothing sincere

Waiting for the next excuse to justify your fears

Your inconsistency is the only thing consistent

and I struggled to find fact in your fiction.

So I force open my eyes,

remember that I can survive.

Accepting that there is a deeper truth in your lies,

In a little while, remnants of this love will only scatter thru my
    mind.

I'll wonder what you're up to, and me,

I'll be hoping that my heart hasn't hardened to your memory;

hoping that you smile when you think of me.

I'll keep busy,

I'll keep living.

Keeping promises that I made from the start.

Remembering how methodically you broke this fragile heart.

See loving is an art.

And you, you are left brain dominant,

a mathematician, subtracting far more than you add.

Doubling my troubles,

you treat love as a fad.

You want to place me in the back of your closet,

Guess I'm last season's hand bag.

I was just an accessory,

something to clutch when you feel bad.

I was that string,

You had me wrapped around your finger.

To remember that love

had taken you thru the ringer.

You were fragile when we met,

But by the end you were callused and mean.

I realized I was just a tool

to resurrect your self esteem.

To wake you up from your nightmare,

But I was never the girl of your dreams.

So sleep well my darling and when you wake I'll be gone.

What you gave me wasn't love.

And this is not a love poem.

Gifts (Haiku)

First he had nothing
Until she gave him her all,
Now she has nothing.

Run On, Sentences

With the precision of an incision

I be makin' decisions

I'm addicted to sentences

And I don't want intervention.

It's murder she wrote

When my pen starts to hemorrhage

When I vent it's vintage.

Freedom is my incentive.

These emotional mixtures

Become modern day scriptures

Isn't it biblical

When disciples join to cypher

Easy to decipher

The writers from the hype men

Who needs beats?

We make hearts weak

when our art form speaks

Poets go harder than rappers

With no rap sheets

Sometimes these lines never lift from the page

But still inclined to uplift and enrage

So imagine when these beast are unleashed on the stage

It's a massacre of silence

Beneath my eye lids

I'm afraid of what will happen if I keep quiet

I been writin' poetry since elementary school days

Imagine feeling like you swallowed a hand grenade

If only someone would listen,

I had so much to say.

Depression almost stole my childhood

So now I speak freely like a child would

Some of these poems are about me.

Some of these poems are about you.

Some folks livin' a lie

So I'm subpoenaed to speak their truth.

I hear it all the time, you poets is crazy

And poetry be my only asylum.

The only force to make the caged bird sing,

and break Maya's silence.

I owe Sally Mae for unused tuition

I was an English major

Just to better my diction

Didn't change my description

Didn't turn fact to fiction

I discovered my true mission

And get paid for my intuition

I promise I'll be writing until they read the benediction.

I promise I'll be writing til they read the benediction.

Circles

We walk around in circles

Never really connect with the Earth, except on the surface

Do you really connect with the God you worship?

Are you open to grow or do you think you're perfect?

Progress makes the process worth it.

I am a blank canvas

Striving to become a master piece

Walking in the Masters peace

Not always right

But always righteous

Haters only exist

in their own abyss

We become shellfish

Trying not to be selfish

Forgetting who your self is,

self destructive

So I live-

For what I'm willing to die for

Heavy weight on my shoulders

But gimme more

GI Jane- in this game,

Demi Moore

Southern trees bare strange fruit

And I speak the same truth

like I hung from the same noose

Ask Harriet why she needed a gun to set slaves loose

Cause some people don't wanna be free

But eye can see

That being subjugated to this system

Is being what they want us to be

And it's no different from slavery.

Emancipate yourself

Understand that knowledge is your greatest wealth

Remember who you are

Be careful with your heart

Seek true healing not just bandages for your scars

Be honest with your intentions

Be truthful even with your presence

Let every person you meet

Be inspired by your essence

If you happen to encounter heartbreak,

Be healed through its lessons

Seems like we walk around in circles

Questioning whether any of this is worth it

You gotta go deeper that the surface

To uncover your divine purpose-

Give Me You (word story)

I wanted your presence.

Not presents-

Natural (Haiku)

I was natural

Before Badu's first CD

But who cared back then?

My Highness (Haiku)

This is my Queendom

Stong, feminine, and royal

God, my only King.

Eye Speak

I speak today for times EYE never spoke

My first poem was a suicide note

So I speak for those who lost hope

And walk on tight ropes

And tote picket signs

I speak, and write, and fight at the same time

Til the finish line

Til this message is no longer confined

Til I become ashes from this grind

This truth be sweet down to the rind

I speak for the good girls and for the whores

who lost their innocence in dark corridors.

The offspring,

Born casualties of this war,

I speak for the dreamers who always read their fortune cookies

The veterans of heartbreak that still rush in like rookies

For the warriors and revolutionaries

The ghetto soldiers who be their own adversaries

I speak for the violence, followed by sirens

Communities are dying

Because of their silence

I speak

For the weak,

who will never find the strength to seek.

Thinking God only wants to meet,

one measly day a week.

Replacing spiritual food

with carnal philosophy.

You are what you eat,

society's meat.

Hunted in these streets

Saturated lies over beats

Digesting fallacy.

Believing fantasy.

I speak because to write-is my birth right.

Pushing through life like it's my birth night

There are words running through my arteries

So to silence me

They would have to slaughter me

And even then,

You would remember me.

And your memory would resurrect me

I speak

Because evolution is contagious

And if self expression became the movement

The results would be outrageous

A brushfire on stages

Enormous if we form this

Alliance of voices

To speak freely,

Then we would truly be,

One nation,

under God,

 indivisible,

with liberty.

I speak.

Identity Theft (Haiku)

The Revolution,

Is not a fad or fashion

It don't have a "look".

Goal Digger (Haiku)

I admit, I live

My life like it is golden

Not quite gold digging

Dear Mimi
(Love and Hiphop)

I'll probably never rock Tom Ford

or designs I can't afford

To afford me access thru superficial doors

With superficial whores

Scoring points on superficial score boards,

Pretending to have it all

while in search for more.

Miss me with your mixtures of wrongly divided scriptures

Where slaves and slave owners

Somehow now,

paint similar pictures

the domestication of our nation,

We've been force-fed fascinations.

Sisters publicly giving head

Now that's modern-day decapitation

So acceptance became means for misinterpretation.

And we ignore the results of sexual fixation

passed down thru generations.

Cause nobody wants to face it.

We were taught to be tasteless,

taught by our rapist.

Miss me with your false alarms

And justification to do me harm.

And when we pay homage,

you say it's voodoo.

But nobody resurrects the stench of strange fruit like you do.

So sisters like Sarah Baartman

lay heavy on my heart man.

Cause these days seem to parallel back then.

And sisters gotta bend over backwards literally,

Like Mimi

To get on T.V.

Like the more I expose,

the more you see me.

And who needs professional training

when this be their reality.

Who deems this demoralizing

when this be her reality.

And who teaches little girls respect,

when this be her reality and this be her mommy

And this be the only God she knows.

And sometimes their reality is driven by these reality shows.

And nobody signs up to have their souls exposed but

But I suppose like there are thorns for every rose.

There are tough choices.

There are lost daughters

There is broken community

We are sleeping, but dreamless.

Desperate,

forgetting that the possibilities are endless.

The audience is insatiable

And thus we asked for this.

So sexuality has become the immunity,

to compromise your dignity.

«But they don't have no awards for that»

So once it's gone,

You can never get it back.

Refunds for your soul,

wasn't written in the contract.

So once it's gone, baby,

you can NEVER-

get it back.

The Time Is...
Write Now (3:18am)

Around this time of night, the writer in me says "Good morning"

With no regard for my mornings

Poems burning in my soul

like hot coal.

Words and sentences,

sentence me to a night in the pen-

Like my thoughts are trapped in the ink.

All I can think-

Is poetry.

Let go of me-

I try to fall asleep

But I fall knee deep in a segment of sentence fragments

and I can't rest til I get these verses of my chest

I come alive when this pen bleeds

I come alive and my thoughts breathe

Verbal selfies

When these perceptions become reflections staring back at me

I must be the Frida Kahlo of poetry.

I need you to SEE what I'm saying

like I painted these poems on your brain.

And even though sleep is calling my name

These poems won't let me rest until

they've been ordained.

Some nights I'm exploring like Dora.

Like my third eye stay watching God, I'm Zora.

And maybe it's me,

Refusing to sleep literally

Cause I refuse to sleep metaphorically.

I figure my people been sleep long enough historically.

So I question my purpose rhetorically.

How ever do you want me?

How ever do you need me?

I am an open book.

I pray to God that you read me.

People are rarely organic

So I'm careful who feeds me.

False Prophets seeking profit so I'm careful who leads me.

I lost my innocence before I knew I owned it.

Almost turned my heart to stone

But I condoned it.

Sometimes out the blue, I remind my 13 year old self that I don't
regret her.

She'll throw a pity party if I let her.

I told her people who make the worse mistakes grow up to be
trend setters.

People only pretend to be perfect, to blend better.

But I rather vent about my vendettas.

No regrets about my endeavors,

And when I finally close my eyes

I rest better.

And stress less.

Ironic how it seems

when you focus on your dreams,

You sleep less.

Like lonely nights in Seattle,

I'm sleepless.

Folks in the Emperors clothes

Profess to be best dressed

But it's nobody left to impress,

When you realize that you're an Empress.

Or a Lioness-

And your pen, keeps you reminded of your greatness.

I'll sleep when the rent ain't due…

Impressions (Haiku)

She frowned so long that
She forgot how to smile and
Her face turned concrete.

Restored (Haiku)

You redeem the kiss-

That was once placed on lips of

The undeserving

Confessions (Part 2)

He shows up empty handed

And that reminds me,

He used to have a hold of my sanity

His system all up in my sol

Like the planets be.

So far away I call him Pluto

He used to be my spades partner

Now I play UNO

And you know,

Solitaire and empty stares into a bassinet

Fighting off regret cause she was far too beautiful to be born of

    my resentment.

She became a symbol of my resilience.

The tenderness of her smile made it hard to become hardened

It wasn't her fault that I had given my flower to someone, who

    had no regard for my garden,

Or that I let my heart place my mind on the back of a milk car-

    ton.

Or when his actions spoke clear

I couldn't hear, and begged his pardon.

Cause you know even when his heart's gone

He can still get a hard on.

So I played Russian roulette,

With my self-respect.

I neglect the inner child

That I failed to protect.

Met him in the V.I.P. Section

Ended up with a C-Section.

Displaced like a lost puppy

at an intersection

Unable to read the subliminal messages,

Even in Braille.

Like pretending the sun is shining even in hail.

Ignoring the fine print and details

subscribing to his issues, wholesale

We sailed,

On a sinking relation-ship

But you will find that your life begins

When your survival skills kick in.

So 18 years later, he still shows up empty handed

And now more than ever,

I understand it.

If you have never been weak,

You will never know what true strength is-

People who only take,

Well, they never learn to give

And the truth is what don't kill you,

inspires you to live.

What didn't kill me,

Inspired me to live.

And we made it.

    -For my daughter, De'sia

Tug Of War

The uncertainties of love have me certain about not wanting it

Chasing it

Haunting it

Ghostlike

Up late night

Good morning heartache

With the rising of the sun

I have loved til I'm numb

Deaf, blinded and dumb

Love is gone by the time I cum

A street bum

I will work for some

Love

My drug of choice, my addiction

Both my healer and

My affliction

My hieroglyphics

Written on my heart

So only you can read

Air through my lungs

that only you can breath

As you be the suffocation

and ventilation

my acceptance and my resignation

both libation and dehydration

I stand for you

And you just stand

Stagnant

Giving me fragments

Cracks in pavement

Part free- part enslavement

Weeds choking our floral arrangement

My hands dirty from toiling

In our garden

I planted sunflowers

So you would know that my heart

Is open

but sometimes we fall in love with the potential,

Distracted by the hoping

Too caught up to realize,

 that we are not growing.

And things are not flowing

Or progressing

We're stressing,

denying that we're digressing.

The more love we invoke

The more hate we provoke

I hate, that I love you,

because illusions never change into proof.

And I am still the delicate flower

choked lifeless by your roots

So I am torn between what I feel and this painful truth.

I hate, that I love you.

But I do.

Between the Lies

Refusing to read between the lines,

I keep believing your lies

And you keep stating the truth

with your actions.

These type of pictures need no
captions.

Sweet Illusion

Truly I miss the blamelessness of my youth

When love was less complex

And I lay trust in an unknown truth.

I thought what I felt was a direct result of what they felt

And the more I believed they was lovin' me,

Well the less I had to love myself

Cause after all, loving them, for me, was effortless.

I am convinced that my lovin' was better before I knew better-

Damn you insight, making me know when it just ain't right

Who wants to exchange being politically correct

For soft kisses to my neck

Even if only temporary

Oh lovin' was good then

Being reeled in,

dropped in the water just before I could breath in

The sensation of sin

The perplexities of honesty is quite the liability

I found no asset

in having to press reset.

If they start living the truth,

Then I must regard it

Making me guarded

And cold hearted

Tell me lies, tell me sweet little lies

Because I prefer illusion over losin'

The truth in its purest form leaves no room for confusion.

But when it became clarified,

I did feel crucified;

the burn of a scar being purified.

Oh I remember love being just what I needed, when I needed it

Never wanted to penetrate the top layers of skin

Never needed to let them in,

Just me, being what they needed me to be

And they, finding the most beautiful ways to give me lies and
  love,

Or pretend that it was,

Can't say I could tell the difference back then

Can't say I really wanted to know the difference.

Sometimes, the truth,

really does hurt.

Reign Drops

We fell in love like raindrops

Emotions precipitate at a fast pace

The Universe seems like a small space

As our journey seems to parallel

From across the world

We mix sweetly like two fruit blending

Into a sauce

We become lost in each other's juices

Creating balance and harmony-

No confusion, but clarity.

This love be free as charity

Staring at each other's duplicates

We match

Like fire waiting to happen.

Like rain falling after a drought

Like the scenic route

Like slowly, the doubt is washed away.

And you promise to stay.

And I promise to let you.

Urgent Care (Haiku)

To love and be loved

Has become an urgency

So we both rush in.

Cussin'

Chile I be cussin"
I don't mean no kinda harm
Jus' a lil seas'nin'
To emphasize my reasonin'.
That's all.

The Spot (Haiku)

One day I found out

That the word woman is spelled

With a "G" like God!

Soul Mate

I know that you are there

Somewhere in a similar head space

On the other side of anxiety

Where patience settles in

Living vicariously through your friends

You live for their stories

Not an ounce of envy

No, no, you've seen the ups and downs of love

And you've had enough

At least for now-

You know that you are not alone just because

There is a beautiful love song on pause

There is a need to allow healing

Layers of our past are pealing

Labels are falling off

Like leaves leave in winter

Grindstone smoothing rugged edges

Leaving just the center

When only the truth is left of you-

When only the truth can get next to you

That's when you know,

That you have taken the time to grow

Confession,

 I am the reason your relationships never seem to go right

Because I have prayed for you day and night

Sometimes, I picture what you will be like

Perfectly designed, no settling this time

Not too flashy

In fact, your message be subliminal

Not for the approval of others

This love will be subtle

Steady and powerful

Of little words

But saying a mouthful

I am child like waiting for you

Smiling at just the thought of you-

Girlish chuckles, biting my knuckles

I know you feel me- in your heart,

 like we are just temporarily apart

Because that's how soul mates are

Like feeling your way through the dark

Like holding wet wood trying to light a spark

I have always felt like something was missing

Walking out the door feeling like I left something

You will be my friend

Storing my secrets in your archives

Hiding me in the security of your protection

Like contraception

I am living, but dying to meet you.

We'll share synonymous stories

Of similar glories

It'll feel like the people we dated were the same

Like we fall victim to similar pain

Similar losses and similar gains

No manipulation,

No games

Like the only thing we haven't exchanged....

Is names

Isolation

Do you know what it feels like to be both lion and lioness?

Both fern and cactus?

Both fulfilled and filled with emptiness

I wear my heart on my sleeve

both intuitive and naive

Sometimes the day I meet them,

I'm preparing for the day they'll leave.

Trying to express my Hi's with the same

courage that it takes to watch them go.

Trying to embrace my highs with the same

humility that I maneuver thru my lows.

I move fearlessly and cautiously.

Isolated and gregariously

My story be both fact and fiction

And sometimes everything I've learned about love

Turned out to be a contradiction, of mysticism

I blame myself for being too forgiving

Therefore not giving enough

Being sweet

Knowing my past has made me bitter

Reiterating the same mistakes

Fear of making any.

I fall back

Into the same regret

My bravery is my greatest weakness.

Do you know what it feels like to be both lion

And lioness?

Being afraid of becoming completely fearless.

Afraid that loving so hard has rendered you loveless,

That caring has made you careless.

Afraid that isolation has made you welcome loneliness.

Isolated and gregarious

My story be both fact and fiction

Both ointment and infliction

And everything I've learned of love,

Turned out to be contradiction

I become antagonist and catalyst

I blame myself for being too forgiving

Therefore not giving enough

Sweet,

While the past has made me bitter

Reiterating the same mistakes

From fear of making any.

I fall forward

In fear of loving backwards

Both unapologetic and with deep regret

Intensely offended over offences that haven't occurred yet.

My bravery is my greatest fear.

Keeping lovers at a distance

While wanting them near.

Seclusion is a means of defense

to avoid false pretense.

Do you know,

what it feels like to be both lion and lioness,

afraid of becoming completely fearless?

Afraid that loving so hard has rendered me loveless,

And caring has made me careless.

This strength has made me weak.

The silence has made me unwilling to speak.

I have become both dominating and submissive

The perpetrator and the victim

I'm afraid that isolation has made me welcome loneliness.

There is darkness

Because I

Refuse to let light in.

There is solitude because I refuse-

to love again.

Simple

Busy is an understatement for this derailment

Things fall apart before they come together

So I'm almost never as calm as I seem.

Never as heroic as in my dreams.

Some days the weight of the world falls on these shoulders

And it would be winter if any colder.

I am the only soldier

In my army.

Air strikes

With no warnings.

Love has felt more like dodging bullets than anything.

Like tension on weak guitar strings,

more chaotic than erotic.

more robotic than exotic.

So tonight,

I need you to uncomplicate

my life.

Slowly, whisper the alphabet in my ear.

Remind me that love,

is supposed to be simple.

Simple Complexities

It must be a complex undertaking, loving an artist.

Being emotionally incarcerated by one whose freedom is what she
is driven by.

Innately requiring more "me-time" than the average willow tree,

born to think analytically, too much structure zaps her energy.

It reminds her of injustice, and slavery

and child abuse and everything inhuman, and you man.

I am guilty.

I may say that I am somewhere else

because curling with a good book just doesn't seem important
enough.

I may say I am somewhere else because writing a poem,

couldn't possibly be important enough. Losing myself is the only
promiscuity I know.

Freedom is like breathing for the artist in me.

She needs the quiet of nothingness more often than most.

You cannot re-cocoon a butterfly.

This one time, I nearly died from compromise.

And so last night—was beautiful.

We lay naked in the purest honesty,

tasting my secrets,

sucking the truth from every lie that's been whispered between

    my thighs,

sucking my breast like you were hungry for my righteousness.

Your arms, were like pythons constricting, and restricting my

    marathon.

I could not run. Oh god, the way you touched me,

held me, spooned me.

In that moment, everything I felt was true,

but I lay there staring at the wall,

thinking of ways to say that I do- not love you.

I much rather you go home,

because this would satisfy me more…in a poem.

Breathe

Sometimes we have to just breathe.

Let things go.

Allow some things out.

Respecting the process of being human,

The way God designed us.

Before we could agree or disagree

It was enough to just be.

All we wanted was to discover.

The womb, used to be enough.

Isolation used to be ok.

No embryo cries because he or she is lonely.

In fact infants cringe at the broken silence.

Slapped and snapped into reality.

The first human expectation is to cry.

The next is to need.

And from that day we forget that the first struggle we faced

was just

to independently,

BREATHE

Daddy's Girl (Lou Lou)

I don't know if it's the experience itself

or the gun you left

that I have to account for my fearlessness

But I walk the Earth like

existing is my birthright

Dudes can't fool girls that know firsthand what a provider looks
   like

We be the royal treatment type.

My hero wasn't trapped in the pages of a comic book.

He was tall, the color of cognac, and ready to change your whole
   life with one look.

He sat in a chair facing the front door

If you knock be ready to explain what you came for

And how long you intended to remain for

A watchman, ready to deliver the pain for-

His tribe.

He promised that my mother would be his only bride.

And that he'd lay down his life for his nine.

And he didn't raise a daughter; he raised a K-9.

He chased Hennessey with the ugly truth

And sometimes his truth was too heavy for me in my youth

But now I understand his urgency

Trying to preserve my innocence

was his only emergency

I was his baby

And he was my inspiration

Al Green, Kenny Rogers, he was my BB King

All I wanted to hear was those down home blues all night long-

Hoping Mama didn't catch me singin' them songs

The living room became a juke joint when Daddy got home.

So I'd surely love to dance with my father again.

I guess heaven couldn't wait for him.

And I imagine my grandmother was there to usher him in.

He taught me that talent ain't nothing without ambition

And don't beg for fish

when you can take yo' ass fishin'.

So although I miss him,

I know he completed his mission.

I was fathered-

in the best way that he knew how.

I just wish I had him with me now.

I just wish....

My Sun

He's quiet,

An introvert

But aware of his surroundings

Says that too much noise is drowning

He prefers silence and solitude

He floats at a higher altitude

His thoughts would impress Socrates

He loves Hip-hop

But hates hypocrisy

There's a hurricane in his brain

Always brainstorming

Global warming can't describe his passion

He subscribes

to a personal understanding

Of Universal things

In silence

He studies human beings

And doesn't speak on what he's seeing

Until the room, is empty.

He can tell you what everyone was wearing

Without staring

Just at a glance

He takes advantage of every chance

To be heard,

without speaking a word.

He's a sponge

Observing and absorbing

He's my son.

His silence speaks volumes.

He is protective

And eclectic

Both humble and electric

A young man with grown man perspective

He is my son.

He is my sun.

 -For Jameel II

Scattered Pieces

She was hoping to see clearer through shattered mirrors

Hoping to find courage

In what provoked her fears

Somehow she feels whole through pain of old and what tears her.

What wears her down to the ground

Familiar sound

Makes her feel found

In the same space that I found her lost

How much did it cost,

to pretend that this picture was a Picasso?

How many tales did it take, to turn her lies to gospel?

I call your name

But to her you are Lot's wife

Gazing into your past hoping what is left will somehow last

As you become sifted sand in an hour glass

Hours pass and I still can't see how our glass became smeared.

How do you forget the taste of your tears,

still staining your cheeks when I got here?

I remember the wounds.

I licked them

Tasted your pain

This was not fiction

But I felt the friction

when you changed positions.

Now you turn ignition.

I become driven away by the same condition.

And now your injury causes my affliction

This pain becomes my addiction

I believed you

When you said I was your prescription

But you never told me you had

side effects.

And that you wanted to see the future in retrospect

You never told me that within our bubble

stood a stunt double.

And that loving you, was creating trouble

Digging thru rubble

Of a troublesome past

That I thought you had gotten past.

These weapons of mass destruction

Trying to mask the repercussions

of loving a succubus

Trying not to see the difference

Between our intentions

Hoping she really loved you and just failed to mention

Between men back then

I hope what she said,

wasn't what she meant.

I hope she meant to touch you

I hope she meant to hold you

I hope she meant that you were beautiful

I hope she meant that you were special

I hope she lied that time,

and not this time.

I hope it's finally your time

and not his time.

I hope this thin line between love and hate

Is really the ocean between faith and fate.

I hope this reality was worth your wait.

I hope her kindness is not just bait.

I hope when this smoke clears, it's not too late.

For your sake

Because in time I'll be healing in the distance

And you'll be –

regretting this decision.

Patterns (Haiku)

I think I'm in love

But then again, this time feels,

Just like the last time.

Dream Lover (haiku)

I want a love to

Lift me- warm me- show me-

That dreams do come true.

Perfect Timing

Not a long time,
but a long time coming.
The race is not over,
But a long time running-
Wiping my brow,
All I remember is right now.
And you are the quench to
my thirst Love,
what I need to keep me going Love,
All this time and still-love
Love to make time stand still-
LOVE
When all the layers have shed
And there is no fabric

Or fabrication

As honest as nakedness

The journey of nations

This, is where two cultures meet

As innocent as our names, rock carved

In the Sycamore tree

With the tenderness of experience,

He rubs her feet.

Like the sun, suspended above us,

The moon, humble enough to wait its turn

But no less significant

Miracles are evidence that God, walks with us.

Who are we to question his ways?

Heaven and Earth in seven days…

Not a long time,

But a long time coming.

Not a long time,

But a long time coming.

Not, a long time,

but perfect-

Timing.

Gin

I imagine you have snooped and sniffed.

Like you sense a difference in your Gin.

Like you sense a difference in your chaser

Like you're no longer penciled in

Like you see the residue of an eraser.

Swiftly you whisk paper.

Trying to pretend that this space, was never given.

You feel a shift in the rhythm.

Who dare to change your station.

Who can endure your intimidation.

Without your permission and interrogation?

I imagine you have sniffed and sniffed and sniffed again

Like you recognize a new fragrance

Somewhat flagrant these fouls

Intentional and narcissistic

Extreme and unrealistic.

This codependency

And small remnants that keep her remembering.

And afraid to

Almost like she is paid to-

Hold on to you.

But

Then each day I sink,

As deep as Indian ink

I know you sit and think

How strong is this link.

Conspiring to inspire and it be carved skin deep.

Just when you've convinced her that I'm not good enough,

She orders another cup.

I be a permanent tattoo.

And I bet you think this poem is about you.

No-

This poem is about Gin.

Chased with something sweet.

Intoxicating.

And unique.

Your deceit, oblique.

But

Memories do fade.

And love is delicious these days.

And well.

You should try dark liquor.

Gin, is my drink of choice.

Dear God (The Secret)

I do not believe that you are flawed

Nor that I am broken or incomplete but rather unique

Positioned and inclined

toward my individual design of constant evolution.

Created to do good yet toil with pollution

I am gifted with the will to choose, to win and lose

And create me,

through this journey of discovery.

Seeing myself as you see me,

In your reflection,

I see my own perfection.

Vital, this connection,

between you and I.

Creator and art form.

You colored me alive and beautiful and powerful.

I am awed.

To be intentionally flawed and given the authority

To become my own masterpiece.

Dear God,

Thank you.

Soul Flower

I feel the shift,

the change in vibration,

I feel the rise,

the turning of pages.

The station changing,

The shattering of glass,

The ground breaking, I am not treading delicately,

I am stomping.

I am gulping, not sipping.

I am not beckoning,

I am reaching.

Hands turned outward.

I am listening

to be heard.

I am evolving

I am turning.

I am changing.

Hoping that I have poured enough of my old self into your memory,

to beg your pardon now, in these days of metamorphosis.

I pray for those who have preyed for me.

Excuse my intuition

And my-

heightened sense of discernment,

Where I hear less of what people say and more of what they meant.

To infinity and beyond

Let's go.

Cutting ties and strings alike.

I let go.

Packing lighter.

Pass my lighter.

Finding gratitude in solitude.

Finding truth in silence.

Meditation

Deeper interpretation

Not becoming hardened,

just taking time to fertilize my own garden.

This flower needs sunlight too.

The Block

They thought 2Pac could save the block

When he couldn't even save hip hop

It's deeper than rap

Minds are trapped in the trap

And these niggas young, gifted and strapped

In all black

Dressed for their own funerals

The block be urinals

For criminals

And it becomes difficult to recognize the victims at the vigils

Camouflaged in this jungle

Who's hunting, and who's the hunted

Who needs help

And who don't want it

So much blood shed

The streets become haunted.

Children become desensitized

To losing lives.

And losing their innocence be their way to survive.

But tender be the tulips of our womb

Sponges soaking air

Living heirlooms

Easily broken

Fragile

Our most prized possessions

Gifts given unto us

Blessings

With thin skin

And feelings

And real thoughts and perceptions

Somehow destroyed by adolescence

We need more love, more unity, more prayer in our community

We need role models that they can see,

standing outside of their T.V.

We need healing and resolution.

Rebuilding and restitution.

Restoration from the lacerations.

Renovation of our nation.

I'm tired of watching our young black boys become-

Products of the environment they come from.

Growing up to be street bums.

But sometimes I see the logic in it.

They are living in a world that we invented,

And maybe our lack of involvement

brings detriment just the same.

Maybe we are setting the example

of doing nothing but expecting change.

Perhaps if they have forgotten their history

It falls on us to remind them.

If in fact this generation is lost,

It falls on us to find them.

Saving My Daughter

See on the flip side,

On the other side of my pride

Right before I almost died

I realized

That giving birth

Was worth the push

And there's always a ram in the bush.

No need to fake it, when you know you can make it.

I remember feeling naked

I-

Remember feeling shaken.

I-

Remember feeling fragile.

But gazing into the eyes of my child

She doesn't realize that love stole my identity.

She sees past this fraud.

See she calls me Mommy

But she thinks I'm God.

So as I lifted her to heaven

Promised I'd give motherhood all I had.

Then God could be my healer. There is a balm in Gilead.

So I recognize the pain of absence.

I know first hand that shits gets real.

But I also taught my daughter,

The truth has nothing to do with what you feel.

I said I know you wonder why your daddy is not here.

Well I think that he's a coward and I think he's filled with fear.

So we don't waste our time on door steps,

Waiting for his return.

We take it all in stride and this be both our lessons learned.

I know it's only mommy

But I've loved you oh so much.

So we embrace what we have

and do not use this as no crutch.

We do not leave room for emptiness.

We do not dwell on absentees.

We learned to be our own super heroes.

This is the making of a Queen.

Winding Roads

I am a woman in human disguise

Complete with curves

As my journey has winding roads

And unexpected turns

And side streets

And back alley.

To find me

I had to search deep

Climb steep

And life ain't been no crystal stair

But I can stare into myself

And be proud

That at my disposal

Both razor and rope

I chose hope

And poetry to set me free

So I float.

And "My Write to Live and Love"

was more than just words I wrote.

It was the answer to a suicide note

It was the answer to a smoke signal

Lost in alienation

Lost in translation

A troubled teen,

who mastered suppression.

Who can dream, when you sleep with depression?

Promiscuity was my act of aggression.

My mama found religion

but there was no booth to confess in.

And no conception of blessin'

When you hate the temple you're dressed in.

And you think where you are,

is where you are destined.

And you can't see pass this moment

So at least if you end it,

It feels like you owned it.

My first poem-was a suicide note.

So every poem since then is a symbol of hope.

I found God for myself at the end of my rope

I learned that He grabs on

When you let go.

So I celebrate my birthdays

Like a national holiday.

Trust me, I went to war for my Independence.

And loving yourself is Labor every Day

I wake up like a kid at Christmas

And it's never about gifts to be bought

It's because some people don't make it past suicidal thoughts

And they jump

Or shoot

Or slice

Or hang

I hear these stories

And realize that I contemplated

them same thangs.

It's really not about a bad choice

It's about listening to the wrong voice.

Or, feeling like you don't have one.

And somewhere between reality and idealism

You feel imprisoned.

So self love be my mantra

And to question be my answer

I operate in a freedom most don't understand

If we met recently,

You almost didn't have the chance.

These days I say exactly what I feel

I'm only here cause He is real.

I'm a poet cause I was destined to be.

Somewhere between these lines

 I found a place where I could be free.

And the loss of innocence

be the gain of Renaissance.

The evolution is obvious in my ambiance

Trying to find me, I found God,

But that's the irony of this quest I'm on.

Being able to look back and the pain is smaller in the distance.

My journey… has winding roads.

This Is

I said I was going on a writing hiatus

But how can I

When society hates us

and rappers degrade us

every chance they get.

Revolutionaries don't take rest.

Haters don't digress.

So why should this Empress.

Why should this feminist.

My people be saturated with European interest.

So I place my imprint

On everything I touch.

I sprinkle these verbs

like herbs

Pass the Dutch

And-

pass the baton

Like Maya lives on,

Like Zora lives on,

cause watching God is all that I know.

Self portraits in these poems

Like Frida Kahlo

Like Aristotle

And the great philosophers

we read about

Like blood in this pen

I'm bleeding out.

Onto the page I

hemorrhage.

Food for thought

My mind's a fridge.

I burn the bridge.

Cause this is a sink or swim situation.

This is my letter of resignation

to the slave master.

This is the remix to the negro spiritual.

This is the rebirth of African rituals.

This is not voodoo.

This is paying homage to the Elders gone before you.

This is not religion of system

This is direct connection

with God

This is the takeover of the Amistad.

This is racial profiling ends tonight.

This is emancipation and preservation of our Civil Rights.

This is exercising my

Civil writes.

This is poetry saving my life.

This is me, no longer waiting to exhale.

This is me pouring all my savings into self publishing and praying
for book sales.

And wishing that as much as I am willing to expose my soul,

that people share my quotes like they share them twirk videos.

Acknowledgments

I would like to thank my children, De'sia Ozzie Ritchey and Jameel Barnes II, for always being supportive of me, and for loving me in a way that keeps me consistently reassured. It's amazing how we balance friendship in all of this. You guys fill in all the spaces. Everything I do is for you. Mommy loves you.

My siblings, David JR, Wanda, Angela, Dwight, Nick, Elliott, Alicia, Alfonso, I cannot say how proud I am to be your baby sister. I pull something different from each of you. As much as there is crazy laughter and fond memories to last me a lifetime, there is inspiration and courage that kept me driven, guided, and guarded through every facet of my life. I love you all.

To my Ritchey, Bowens, Kinchen, Haugabrook, and Royal family near and far, thank you for being an intricate part of my life and growth. I love you more than I can ever say.

To my Carol City Chiefs and all of my Dade County folks, we are…a family. Thank you for taking each of my products to another level. Your support is amazing, and I'm proud to be est. in Dade County.

To all the POETS who have supported, pushed, and encouraged me to complete this project. I am forever grateful that we crossed paths and that you chose to walk with me on this journey. I cannot thank you enough. It would take years to name you all, but GS Cole, and Will Seri'us, ya'll are everything!

Analogy Smith, some days you believe in me far more than I believe in myself. I love you more than I could ever say.

Eullys Jewelz Hinnant III, when I think back, to the beginning, I see you there, booking me for shows behind my back! It was the greatest act of friendship and admiration I had ever experienced. I love you.

Terri Meredith, your contribution to this project is both touching and amazing. I am forever grateful. Your contribution to my heart as a friend and to my life as an artist has exemplified truth and justice of self. I am forever inspired by you.

Now to my Facebook and Instagram fam …you guys keep me encouraged. Thank you for "liking" and "sharing" my poems and helping me spread my writing across a World Wide Web. Your support is priceless. I am humbled and moved by you. You inspire me more than I could ever express.